Marvelous Messages From Your Childhood

Thirteen Traits that Reveal

Your Hidden Potential and Empower You to

Answer the Calling of Your Heart

Jamie Linn Saloff

SENT
BOOKS

SENT BOOKS

Marvelous Messages From Your Childhood.
Copyright © 2020, 2023, Jamie Linn Saloff. All rights reserved.

No part of this work may be reproduced in any manner whatsoever or otherwise be copied for public or private use, without written permission of the publisher, other than for "fair use" as brief quotations embodied in critical articles and reviews. Purchase only authorized electronic editions, and do not participate in or encourage electronic piracy of copyrighted materials. Your support of the author's rights is appreciated. Requests for permissions should be addressed to:

Sent Books
P. O. Box 339
Edinboro, PA, 16412

Cover image, Homunkulus28 /iStockPhoto.com. Used with permission.
The Ugly Duckling quotes by Hans Christian Andersen, from J.H. Stickney translation, ©1886, 1914, Ginn and Company.
H.C. Andersen photo, The Royal Library, Dansk, used with permission.

Print: ISBN 978-1-7325300-5-8
Ebook: ISBN 978-1-7325300-6-5
LCCN: 2019917234
First edition, ©2020, 2023. v. 1.04
Copyright information available upon request.

In memory of

Kerry Stuart Kennedy

a Swan, a visionary, and

a giving, kindhearted soul.

Visit Jamie's website at:
https://www.MarvelousMessages.com

"I know you have your doubts.

You have been through something

that no one should ever go through.

You're going to be okay."

Dr. Daniel Jackson to Col. O'Neill,
Stargate SG1, "The Abyss"

Contents

Your Childhood Is Important 2

When Fairy Tales Are True 5

Thirteen Traits You May Have That Could Transform

    Your Life 9

Activating Your Inner Potential 43

Next Steps 61

About Jamie Saloff 63

Last Thoughts 65

Difficult childhood?

The unique and trying situations
you experienced as a child,
at a time when you were the most impressionable,
programed your mind with survival tactics
that kept you going
through whatever trials you faced.

Now, these same tactics
can become the traits you need
to persevere through life's challenges and
succeed where others fail.

Found amidst many leaders, celebrities, sports stars,
musicians, artists, and other iconic luminaries
are thirteen traits often formed
during childhood's difficult, early years.

Ironically, those who may have been hit the hardest
are often the ones with the greatest tendency
to carry all thirteen.

Are you one of them?

Your Childhood Is Important

The thirteen traits described herein are a part of an ingrained toolset found in many highly successful people. These skills occur in individuals who lived through an unusual or difficult childhood and were formed as part of a subconscious survival system.

Early on, I didn't realize just how many of us acquire these skills. But some years ago, I created an online quiz asking visitors to select all the traits they recognized in themselves. While I expected responders to have a random number of the traits, that's not what happened. Almost all cited not one or two or three, but all thirteen—13 out of 13. This flabbergasted me. I never expected that result.

Your childhood was. . . well, your childhood. And however good or bad it might have been, it has shaped you into who you are today and empowered you as to who you can be tomorrow.

Looking back on my youth, I had very few aspirations. I merely wanted to survive and move on to adulthood, where I hoped-prayed-wished that what pained me as a child would end. I believed that, as an adult who could make my own decisions, I could create a better life, a life that measured up more closely to my imagined ideals.

Growing up in an era of racial riots, Watergate, the Vietnam War, Kent State shootings, and many other disruptive events, I worried about the state of the world. I went through periods of depression, considered running away, and contemplated suicide on several occasions. I wrote in my diary at age fifteen that I didn't expect to live past thirty.

As a youth, I spent hours writing countless journal entries and making numerous lists, always wanting to decode the mysteries of my life. Mostly, I wanted to know how to better myself. I wondered, "How do I make the most of my life?"

I desperately wanted to ensure my life had value. Part of this desire stemmed from having a sister who died before she could explore all the opportunities of life. We never got to meet. Thus, I felt compelled to make the most of my life to also honor hers.

As I grew up, married, had children, and faced all that adulthood brings. I left behind what few aspirations I may have had. They were like boxes of old photographs forgotten on a dusty shelf. I pushed aside all my childhood dreams, which seemed pretty impossible anyway.

When my doctors diagnosed me with cancer, I thought my yet young life was over. I began to regret having left behind my dreams—however small they may have seemed. I knew I hadn't just let myself down, but my sister as well. I wanted a second chance to make them come true.

After I recovered from cancer, that chance reopened for me. Even so, my first steps forward were very small. In those days, I had very little confidence and low expectations.

Nevertheless, I knew by then that we all have a tremendous inner potential to actualize the deepest callings of our heart, and that we all carry within ourselves the necessary tools to overcome the challenges and roadblocks standing in our way. Especially when we are young, most of us have little or no idea of the ultimate, marvelous beings we could turn out to be.

At first, I had difficulty explaining the thirteen traits to others. They would nod, pretending they understood, but I could see in their eyes they did not. Most didn't believe *they* might really have unlimited potential. Others simply dismissed my ideas and my ability to know anything about it.

I didn't yet know how to reach them or how to clearly explain what I had come to understand.

But, then, I had a breakthrough...

When Fairy Tales Are True

Early in 19th century Denmark there lived a man who came from a broken home. He had known poverty, rejection, lost loves, and abuse. It had been rumored he was a bastard son of the king (but that has never been proven).

Sent to a school for poor children, he was forced to support himself until he left town and country at age fourteen to seek his fortune.

For a while, he tried his hand at singing and acting, but when his voice changed, he was encouraged by a colleague to try writing. He published his first story in 1822. He was befriended by a theatre director who advised him to go to school and persuaded the king to partially cover the expense.

Despite receiving an education, it was in school that he spent some of his darkest days. Not only was he discouraged from writing, he was so harshly treated that he left in a state of depression. It was at this juncture he wrote a poem called *The Dying Child*.

These true-life happenings are important because their effects are reflected in the stories he later wrote, including *The Little Mermaid, The Emperor's New Clothes, The Princess and the Pea, The Little Match Girl, The Snow Queen,* and *Thumbelina*. He also wrote novels, travelogues, plays, and poetry.

Hans Christian Andersen, ©Dansk Royal Library, used with permission.

Among his fairy tales, one gem stands out, *The Ugly Duckling*. It is from this tale we begin to learn of the thirteen traits which shape our early lives and bestow upon us tremendous potential.

Hans Christian Andersen (1805-1875) or "H. C.," as he liked to be called, was able to see inside the heart of the ugly duckling in his story because he had lived that type of life himself.

Woven within his stories, the reader finds clues to H. C.'s fears, character, longings, and his ability to rise above it all to become one of the world's most beloved children's writers.

It is from his life's story and the tale of *The Ugly Duckling* that we are able to see our own potential, despite any hardships we may now be facing or may have faced in our past.

As I re-read *The Ugly Duckling* as an adult, I took the story to heart because I too had lived in the shadows as a misfit, outcast, ugly duckling. While my life had been tremendously different from that of H. C.'s, as I read his story, I found many similarities entwined within the *influences* directing our lives.

More importantly, as I identified and wrote about these traits, my research and deeper explorations revealed how many of today's leaders, celebrities, sports stars, musicians, artists, and other iconic luminaries had also experienced these traits too.

A pattern emerged...

I could see how these life effects were more than just hardships, but rather life-changing influences that could empower us to outstanding success, happiness, and deep, inner fulfillment.

The more I studied the story, the more I began to clarify the traits brought about by these experiences and their effects. I wrote them down and began telling others about them, always talking about "the Swan effect" or relating to those who had become empowered by these traits as "Awakened Swans."

Of course, most people just looked at me as if I had grown two heads. But I also saw there were many who had these traits and didn't realize how to utilize them to their advantage.

And the best part?

Most of these traits are very common!

Often the difficult challenges we struggled against, especially in the younger years of our life, become the catalysts we need now to leap forward. We simply did not realize at the time just how valuable these challenges might be.

The resulting thirteen traits are key influences in transforming an "ugly duckling" into a "Swan." The more these traits have influenced your life, the greater your potential to realize the deepest desires of your heart.

How many of the thirteen traits are prevalent in your life?

Thirteen Traits
You May Have
That Could
Transform Your Life

As previously mentioned, the following thirteen traits are derived from H. C.'s story of *The Ugly Duckling*.

Quotes are taken from an original 1866 translation found in the public domain. Many of today's modern translations change or leave out key points in the story.

See how many of these traits you can relate to.

1. Did You Have an Unusual Childhood?

"Unusual" is a subjective term but includes situations such as:

- Separation from a parent
- Severe or life-threatening Illness
- Abuse
- Death of a family member
- Subjected to the tragedies of war/terrorism/crime
- Exposed to domestic violence
- Transient lifestyle
- Extreme poverty
- Trauma/fear/worry
- An odd awareness or life-shaping moment in time
- Unique lifestyles widely different from the "norm"

If any trait is telling of the Swan phenomena, it's this one. It seems that nothing about the ugly duckling's childhood was normal. Abused and ridiculed, shocked by murder, threatened by dogs, poverty-stricken, and alone, yet he made his way.

Look up the bio of your favorite celebrity, sport's star, or other high-achiever, and you will likely find hints of this trait.

My childhood included many unusual circumstances including my sister's death; my father's debilitating illness, loss of a leg, and early demise; a generation gap of eighteen years between my brother and myself; multiple moves to new cities and schools; and more, all making it difficult for me to fit in. I grew up loving all misfit stories:

- *Rudolph the Red-Nosed Reindeer*
- *Charlie Brown*
- *Square Pegs* (yes, that really was a tv show)
- *The Point* (a lovely animated story set to music by Harry Nilsson)
- *Goonies*
- *The Breakfast Club*
- *Beetlejuice, The Addams Family, The Munsters*
- *Nightmare Before Christmas*
- *Napolean Dynamite*
- (and of course) *The Ugly Duckling*

And there are so many more. . . maybe it's because there are so many of us out there who have fallen into this misfit category. I think all the *X-men* and superheroes are also "Swans." Just think of their beginnings. They are all created out of some strange or unusual happening.

If you had an unusual or difficult childhood, you more than likely are packed with potential and have the skills you need to fulfill your deepest and most heartfelt dreams. The framework you grew up in has gifted you with the talents you need going forward.

It doesn't matter if you grew up in a loving home surrounded by a supportive family or have sworn off a whole list of rogue relatives you hope to never hear from again, the mold has been cast and you are on your way.

2. Are You Lucky to Be Alive?

In the whole of your life, how many times might you have died?

- ▷ a near-miss car crash
- ▷ the illness/injury that should have taken your life
- ▷ the silly/dangerous stuff you did when you were younger
- ▷ that close-call
- ▷ a dark threat
- ▷ a faulty electrical outlet
- ▷ a terrible storm
- ▷ and more... (you know what I mean)

And yet, you're still here.

Amazing, isn't it?

I call this Divine Providence.

I find that many of us have faced a life-threatening situation at some point in our lives, though, in some cases, it may have been a minor incident we may have pushed aside or even forgotten.

H. C. doesn't explain how the ugly duckling's egg ended up in the wrong nest. (A greylag goose has an inbred instinct to push any round object back into its nest, so perhaps H. C. took a writer's liberty to add this trait to ducks.) He does infer that it happens frequently because, as the Old Duck complains:

> *"I've no doubt it's a Guinea fowl's egg. The same thing happened to me..."*

Divine Providence means that despite all odds and a series of unlikely circumstances, you are still here. My dictionary defines "providence" as "God's divine will." You have a calling, a purpose, a meaning of presence. This purpose is not just your ultimate calling, but also all the people's lives you touch along the way.

Think about that for a moment. Despite any misfortunes or hardships you have faced—and I know you have—you are still here.

Divine Providence means you still have something important to do. I encourage you to find out what it is, begin doing it, and keep doing it by listening to the calling within. *(I will explain more about this later.)*

3. Do You Need to Feel Safe?

People who have experienced terror, trauma, and/or unrest may have a deep-seated desire to feel safe in all they do. H. C. said of the ugly duckling:

> *"And so he lay quite still, while the shot rattled through the rushes, and gun after gun was fired over him.*
>
> *It was late in the day before all became quiet, but even then the poor young thing did not dare to move."*
>
> *He waited quietly for several hours and then, after looking carefully around him, hastened away from the moor as fast as he could."*

This safety mechanism may show itself in how you interact with others. When making plans, you may always have a silent "backup plan" for your "escape," or be noncommittal.

This trait may manifest as a need to control your surroundings and circumstances. (A sense of "being in control" offers a sense of security even though it may only be perceived so in the mind.)

However, if you have this trait, this means that, typically, when you do commit to something, you are all in. And, if you like control, you may be a good planner because you have thought through many-a-potential scenario and have a plan of action for whatever may occur. You may be the hero in a situation because you are aware of things others are not.

4. Do You Prefer to "Fly" Your Own Way?

Are you comfortable being yourself, even if that means acting differently from the crowd?

Are you able to express a difference of opinion with ease while in conversation?

Do you express your personality by the way you dress, how you speak, and/or by how and where you live?

In the story, the hen tells the ugly duckling:

> *"...you are a chatterer, and your company is not very agreeable. Believe me, I speak only for your good. I may tell you unpleasant truths, but that is a proof of my friendship. I advise you, therefore, to lay eggs and learn to purr as quickly as possible."*
>
> *"I see you don't understand me," said the duckling."*

When you see a fellow walking down the street with a spiked mohawk, black goth attire, 80% of his body covered in tattoos and piercings, all while carrying a boa constrictor around his neck, those extremes remind me of the unique ways people outwardly express themselves.

While I don't dress in that manner, I do say that I "decorate myself like a Christmas tree." I wear rings on every finger (some multiple), lots of bracelets, sparkling shoes, flowing scarves, and adorned hair. I'm not afraid to wear bright colors or stand out in the crowd.

How do you express yourself?

What is it about Awakening Swans that makes many of them outspoken and outwardly unafraid to show they are different?

This trait seems to puzzle people the most as it appears very contradictory to the other traits. Yet, those with this trait will tell you it's true. Many may have tried repressing their beliefs and found they couldn't.

> *"...the duckling sat in a corner, feeling very low-spirited; but when the sunshine and the fresh air came into the room through the open door, he began to feel such a great longing for a swim that he could not help speaking of it."*

In sixth grade, my bigoted French teacher acted out violently against a particular student in the class. While all the students were horrified by what she did, no one wanted to tattle on the teacher.

Despite being shy and quite withdrawn, I decided I would not attend class with a woman of that nature. I found I could not hold back my feelings about it. The school principal attempted to belittle me and scare me into going back, but I refused. Because of that, most of the other kids were afraid to associate with me. I was too different.

As a misfit, it doesn't matter how you look or what you do. There is no longer any pressure to follow any fad or trend. Even if I had, it wouldn't have mattered. I had already been typecast. Wearing the correct designer clothes or owning the latest electronic doodad wasn't going to change that.

Children (and many adults) are quick to label and blacklist others who they fear or don't understand.

Being an outcast comes with a special kind of freedom allowing people with this trait to release a pent-up piece of themselves. It's a tremendous advantage to have the ability to be true and authentic to one's self. Being so opens the door to a deeper ingenuity, creativity, spontaneity, and other means allowing you to crash through previously set limitations.

People with this trait carry a kind of unseen magnetism. Others almost immediately sense that you are different.

Regardless of how they react to it, if they can sense it, then being a "Swan" must be something really wonderful.

> *"... live people ignore the strange and unusual. I, myself, am strange and unusual."*
>
> Lydia, in *Beetlejuice*

5. Growing Up, Did You Wonder if You Were Adopted?

While you were growing up, even if all evidence said otherwise, did you ever wonder if you were adopted?[1]

Whether your parents were good or bad, loving or cruel, they were your parents. Yes, they made mistakes in your upbringing, they all do—some more than others. However, they gave you several things that cannot be denied.

The first is your heritage, that rich field of ancestry that flows back through time, throughout your bloodline, as far back as the beginning of time.

The second is their teaching of that heritage through their interactions while you were growing up. Whether you embraced it or rejected it, this becomes the framework from which you built your life.

As we begin to awake and mature, we form our own values and beliefs, some of which contradict what our parents were taught. It's not uncommon for us to question why our parent's traditions, customs, and habitual traits are what they are.

That is why some of us may find ourselves wondering if we were adopted, especially if most everyone else in the family seems oblivious to the opposing views we hold so dear.

---

[1]. If you really *were* adopted, you still glean influences from your surrogate family.

Children come into the world not only to learn from their heritage but also to expand the beliefs of those who came before. If you've ever seen *Fiddler on a Roof*, that is exactly what happens.

These differences may come in the form of the cattle farmer who raises a vegetarian, a Republican family whose daughter becomes a Democrat, a Christian family whose son is gay, and so and on.

As we grow and develop our own values and style, we test the beliefs and values that our parents held so dear. Depending on the family, conflicts may arise.

> *"The duckling thought that others might hold a different opinion on the subject, but the hen would not listen to such doubts."*

As we recognize our beliefs are different, we begin to question how we could possibly see the world so differently from those who bore us. It can cause us to doubt our parentage when, more often than not, we truly are their offspring, we are just bucking the predisposed family system.

> *Mama Duck: "...See how well he uses his legs, and how erect he holds himself! He is my own child, and he is not so very ugly after all, if you look at him properly."*[2]

Your unique view of the world is one of the ways you are able to rise above the rest.

---

2. One might contend the ugly duckling was adopted due to a swan's egg being in a duck's nest. Yet, Mama Duck truly hatched (birthed) him.

from Your Childhood | 21

6. Do You Find It Hard to Make a Decision?

Do you struggle to make decisions, particularly when they are life-changing? Some of the more common decisions include:

- job/career change
- exiting a relationship
- choosing a college/career
- committing to a long-term relationship
- choosing a new house or home
- deciding to move across the country or overseas

Difficult decision-making may trickle down into the mundane including deciding what to wear, where to eat, and more. And sometimes we forget that *not* making a decision is still a decision.

How is it possible to make an important decision if you are living in an environment where any conflicting choice will be criticized, analyzed, disagreed with, or even possibly punished for—physically and/or emotionally? How can the logical mind defend against this?

Isaac Asimov's famous story *I, Robot* explains how robots are programmed so as to never cause harm—are not our own minds instinctively designed to protect us from hardship whenever possible?

Therefore, our decision process becomes twisted in a logical loop as it tries to find the safe ground between what will cause discomfort to the body-mind and what will bring happiness.

The result in this type of situation is that we may be unable to find a logical answer, thus making a decision becomes difficult.

> "...the poor little thing did not know where to go, and was quite miserable because he was so ugly as to be laughed at by the whole farmyard."

The only way out of the loop is to make decisions based on the purest, deepest heart's calling—the intuitive gut knowings, which *physically feels right* but may ruffle others' feathers.

As long as you stand before the mirror of others' scrutiny, your logical mind will often thwart your decision-making process.

Regardless of your decisions, someone else is bound not to like them, therefore it's best to seek what will further your life, rather than to please anyone else.

This is a delicate balancing act often faced by people with this trait. It isn't always easy or possible to go against the opposition against you. Choose your battles. Focus on decisions that really matter to the quality of your life and don't worry about the smaller matters where you may have to give in.

7. Do You Struggle to Lose Weight?

Do you carry extra weight, finding that no matter what you do you cannot drop that extra 20 - 30 - 40 - or more pounds?

Continuing from the conflict just explained, people with this trait tend to form an extra layer of protection designed to keep them from the harmful blows (physical or emotional) that are continually hurled at them.

> *"...bless me, what a queer-looking object one of them is; we don't want him here"; and then one flew out and bit him in the neck.*

> *"...he is so big and ugly. He's a perfect fright," said the spiteful duck, "and therefore he must be turned out. A little biting will do him good."*

Note, some of these blows we wield upon *ourselves* with over-analytical, self-criticisms and falsely-accepted beliefs.

In addition, we must find freedom from the strife and abuse in our lives, whether self-inflicted or incited by others. This may mean escaping the conflict or standing up to it. *(The latter is more powerful, but sometimes the former is the only respite.)*

Weight also becomes a visible symbol of our unmoving stance. It gives us the power and strength to remain firm at the core level of who we are. The more we move into being true to our deepest inner selves, the more our body is freed from unnecessary weight.

8. Do You Keep Getting Sick?

Have you struggled with chronic pain, ailments, disorders, or illness now or in the past?

Do you ever get the feeling that just as you heal from one thing something else occurs?

Do you suffer from a painful disorder or recurring symptoms?

Common ailments include:

- migraine headaches
- chronic sinus, allergies
- digestive issues
- painful, old injuries
- backache
- knee, hip, or ankle pain
- shoulder problems
- neck pain
- anxiety
- Chronic Fatigue, Adrenal Fatigue, Fibromyalgia,
- and many more...

> *[The ugly duckling] became exhausted at last and lay still and helpless, frozen fast in the ice... Early in the morning, a peasant who was passing by saw what had happened. He broke the ice in pieces with his wooden shoe and carried the duckling home to his wife. The warmth revived the poor little creature...*

Physical symptoms are often the body's signal that you've repressed your inner voice. We go to the doctor and receive treatment. For a time, we are made well. But we are treating the symptom and ignoring the underlying cause.

When we bypass the emotional connection, after a time, either that symptom returns or a new one crops up. The body always knows when we are answering the call and being true to our authentic self.

To break through recurring symptoms, we must discover their underlying meaning. When we do so, we are shown the ways and means to accelerate our forward progress.

There are ways[1] to dig deeper into the workings of these nagging symptoms and to discover their underlying connections to our flight path. This is one of the ways I healed my life after facing cancer and several other life-threatening situations.

---

1. Read *Marvelous Message from Your Body*. where I explain one such way.

Have You ACEd It?

I've been writing about "Swans" for years in my journals, my notes, and my books. But there were others discovering this in their own way. It hasn't all been just fairy tales and speculation, there are some real scientific studies out there, and they are beginning to gather attention.

Early in 2019, I read Donna Jackson Nakazawa's, *The Last Best Cure*. In it, she talked about her discovery of ACEs. Although the initial ACE study was begun in 1995, I'd never heard of it. (Neither had Donna when she started writing her book.)

ACE is *Adverse Childhood Experiences* and studies about it have shown how children who experience physical or emotional trauma in their lives are more likely to face physical illness in their adult years. Donna's doctor, Anastasia Rowland-Seymour tells her in the book:

> *"The early trauma you experienced sparked neural pathways and a pattern of hormone and chemical cascades that have impacted you on a cellular level for decades."*

Later, Nakazawa learns:

> *"Children who have a parent die, face emotional or physical abuse, experience childhood neglect, or witness severe marital problems between parents are more likely to develop cardiovascular disease, cancer, lung disease,*

diabetes, headaches, and, as we've seen, autoimmune disorders like multiple sclerosis and lupus. Facing difficult circumstances in childhood increases your chances of having chronic fatigue syndrome as an adult sixfold. . . ."

Rowland-Seymour further explains:

"But what you really need to translate for people—those for whom Western medicine has done all it can—is this: all the science is pointing to the fact that your brain is your last best cure."[1]

Or, in other words, you hold the power within to transform your life!

Nakazawa, who suffers from an autoimmune disease, turned to meditation, yoga, and acupuncture in conjunction with traditional medical treatments. Through her year-long practice of these things, she writes of how she begins to find relief.[2]

A variety of other studies abound, as well as the ever-increasing DNA research showing the effects of childhood trauma and their resulting adult lives. To learn more, Google terms such as "generational trauma" or "epigenetics."

---

1. Quotes from: *The Last Best Cure*, Donna Jackson Nakazawa, ©2013, Hudson Street Press, the Penguin Group.
2. You can take the ACE test yourself at www.AcesTooHigh.com where you will also find news reports, research links, and more.

9. Do You Want to Run Away?

Do you sometimes have the urge to run away (get away / stay away) from everything and everyone?

You may even have a mental list of what you will take, where you will go, and how you will make your "escape." This may be a passing fancy that has come and gone throughout your life or something you actually did at some point in the past.

The ugly duckling ran away:

> *"The ducks pecked him, the chickens beat him, and the girl who fed the poultry pushed him with her feet. So, at last, he ran away, frightening the little birds in the hedge as he flew over the palings."*

Maybe you don't see it as running away. Perhaps you are a drifter or one who moves a lot from job to job or state to state. People with this trait seem to be searching for something and don't always know what it is that is missing from their lives. They just know that something just doesn't feel right. They haven't yet found where they fit so they move on.

For some, this manifests as someone who is an introvert. They are simply more comfortable alone or in like-company doing things they enjoy.

Still, others run to escape conflict, distress, or even harm. Living within an oppressive environment causes conflict and stress, sometimes escalating to the point where the pressure becomes unbearable. When the pressures of conflict escalate, people with this trait long to escape.

In the story, the ugly duckling runs away a lot. He runs away from home. He runs from the moors and the hunters. He runs from the old woman, cat, and hen. He runs from the farmer, the farmer's wife, and their kids. He seems to always be on the run.

This need to run can also be self-imposed. Sometimes what we are running from is our confused state of mind. Running away doesn't fix that. (Although, being in a vulnerable place, we may not yet be able to stand up against our oppressor and escape may be our only reprieve. Such was the case of when the old woman considered eating the little duck!)

It can be difficult to remain true to your heart while remaining within the confines of your upbringing. Those who stand firm and express their true identity may not only free themselves from their limitations but may also change the beliefs of those around them. At that point, you are no longer an "ugly duckling," you have fully awakened and transformed into a "Swan."

Many people with this trait often transform so quickly and so many times that they always appear to be transitioning to some new incarnation of themselves. They seem to experience a constant self-evolution and wide array of interests. . . that's not a bad thing, even if others see it as walking away from things unfinished. Once the desired learning has been grasped, people with this trait simply move forward to the next thing.

10. Have You Ever Wished Your Life Was Over?

Have you ever experienced suicidal thoughts, particularly as an adolescent; or simply wished that you would quietly pass away?

Though you won't likely find it in a politically correct children's story, the older, original versions retain how the ugly duckling desired for his life to end. He did not see that the best of his life was about to begin.

> *"I will fly to these royal birds, and they will kill me because, ugly as I am, I dare to approach them. But it does not matter; better to be killed by them than pecked by the ducks, beaten by the hens, pushed about by the maiden who feeds the poultry, or starved with hunger in the winter."*

Most modern-day fairy tales removed these types of statements from children's books because they fear if children see them, it may encourage them to take action on those kinds of thoughts. I believe that knowing others have had such thoughts and fought through them to a positive end, might be an encouragement to press on through dark times.

People with this trait who suffer from a lingering misery can be drug down like a lead weight in water. Depression may set in. (If severe, seek medical treatment.) Unless a person has walked through depression—as I have—they do not understand how a person with "everything" cannot find happiness, and, if their situation is bleak, then it's all the worse.

What happens then is the desire to run away suddenly means not just from others, but also from life itself.

But wait!

This is merely a symptom of not responding to the inner call, or upon hearing it, feeling so distraught over not being able to access it. An overwhelming desire to give up may arise. (Fight it! Get help if needed!)

Please, please, please, let me assure you since I have traversed this path, it does get better, especially if you allow the transformation to occur. I can vouch for this on many levels, and I assure you that it's not just true for me, but for everyone.

I first contemplated suicide around age fourteen. There was the time I considered taking an entire bottle of pills, the time I held a knife to my wrist (but someone stopped me), the time I nearly jumped out a window (I thought it would be too painful), and the time I simply pleaded with God to take my life (I tell that story in my book, *Hatch – A Change Your Life Guide*.) But I'm still here ... thankfully.

I guarantee that you are here for a reason, you are important, and your divinely-given purpose is absolutely necessary, however insignificant you might feel in this state.

During one of my low points after almost dying from an illness, I wondered why I had survived. I didn't want to be here anymore. A friend sat me down and said:

"I am not going to complete your mission for you, you have to do it. I'm already doing all I can. It's up to you to fulfill whatever purpose you came here to do."

Something about the way he said it sank deep inside me and connected with whatever subconscious knowledge I had about my calling in life.

Now I see how far I've come, how much I've accomplished, and how many lives that I've touched. I know he was right. Who knows what else I may yet do before my time finally ends.

Who knows what YOU may yet accomplish.

Every day is a new opportunity. Our situations can change in an instant—even when that seems impossible. Grab up your life with both hands and use each day as best as you can.

> National Suicide Prevention Hotline
> 1-800-273-8255

11. Are You Under the Influence?

When we have been exposed to those who are not of like mind, and whose disposition has been darkened by their hardships, they give their opinions to you to wear like a heavy coat.

> *"...I wish his mother could smooth him up a bit; he is really ill-favored."*

> *"He has remained too long in the egg, and therefore his figure is not properly formed;"*

> *"You are exceedingly ugly," said the wild ducks..."*

> *"Can you raise your back, or purr, or throw out sparks?" said the cat. "No." "Then you have no right to express an opinion when sensible people are speaking."*

The more we live in and are exposed to an environment of negativity about the world, our situations, and ourselves, the more we begin to accept other people's opinions about us and claim them as our own. So often had the ugly duckling been told he was ugly, he believed it to be true.

> *"...at the same moment a large, terrible dog passed quite near him. His jaws were open, his tongue hung from his mouth, and his eyes glared fearfully. He thrust his nose close to the duckling, showing his sharp teeth, and then 'splash, splash,' he went into the water, without touching him."*

> *"'Oh,' sighed the duckling, 'how thankful I am for being so ugly; even a dog will not bite me.'"*

Even once we exit that environment, those ghosts of how we see ourselves linger on in our psyche's closet.

> *"Poor ugly creature, how gladly he would have lived even with the ducks, had they only treated him kindly and given him encouragement."*

Most of us do not have an inkling of the potential within nor the heights that we can reach. It's hard to throw off the ugly duckling cloak we have worn for so long.

When we do, and when we allow ourselves to be seen for who we really are aside from the naysayer's opinions, we not only are able to step into a transformed self (a.k.a., the Swan), but we also remove a heavy burden from our minds and hearts.

> *"The new one is the most beautiful of all, he is so young and pretty." And the old swans bowed their heads before him."*

Perception is everything. Remember that from the time the ugly duckling had been born, and even before, no one had ever told him he was a swan. In fact, he had never even seen a swan, except during one passing moment where he happened to see a flock just as it took to flight. All he ever knew was what others told him, and what they told him was that he was an "ugly duckling." Yet, he never was an ugly duckling because he wasn't a duck!

What have others said about you?

Transformation began for the ugly duckling when he changed his perception—something that happens in an instant—something that didn't change who he always was, but allowed him to see—for the very first time—what he had never recognized about himself before—he was a "Swan."

The ugly duckling didn't change—how he saw himself did.

That change was more powerful than you can ever imagine, it was more powerful than magic, more life-changing than plastic surgery, more transforming to who he would be the rest of his life than winning the lottery; more life-releasing than running away.

So often before, his perception of himself had been distorted by the beliefs he put on himself. Yet, it could not have been possible for him to make this leap had he not been exposed to others like himself. The only way he could break the old mirrored images of himself was to be in a position where new ones could take their place.

Learn to understand that you are born of a "Swan's egg." Truly, you are a "Swan," you just have to see yourself for who you really are not the "you" others have placed on you.

Look for others who are doing what you long to do or who will support you in your quest. Let their wisdom and encouragement help transform you into who you truly are and quested to be.

12. Is Your Heart Calling You to Action?

What do you dream of doing? What is the call to action that keeps tugging at your heart?

You may have been longing to do this for years or maybe it's something new you just can't get out of your head. Even if it seems impossible, you've noticed, the tug doesn't go away.

The heart's call to action is a key influence for becoming a Swan.

In *The Ugly Duckling* story, the call of the heart is the one thing that no one can take away from the downtrodden, little bird. With no other resources available, his pleading heart led him to far more than he ever could imagine—that of being a Swan.

Stepping into your calling can be difficult at first. This is when all of your protective senses go into high gear, warning you of the dangers ahead. Those dangers are the hurdles that are blocking your way, roadblocks that you must break through if you hope to succeed.

In addition, as you step toward that which you desire to do the most, you'll find you're immediately met with challenges. Accept them as a sign that your desire is true to your path. Know too that the skill set you need to overcome this challenge already resides within you. By vanquishing each challenge one by one, you will evolve and enhance your heart's desire further.

13. Do You Immerse Yourself in Activity?

Do you fit into any of the following categories: Workaholic, shopaholic, Internet addict, TV, movie or book addict, food addict, or even an alcoholic or drug addict?

Do you dive in deep when you do something?

Why are you driven to keep busy or to distract your mind?

> *"...he was obliged to swim about on the water to keep it from freezing, but every night the space on which he swam became smaller and smaller."*

This *Ugly Duckling* quote shows him obsessively swimming in circles, something he felt necessary for survival. Throughout the story, we also learn how he continues to move from place to place, never really finding anywhere he is comfortable, so he keeps moving.

When we keep busy or hold our mind in an altered state, we drown out the voice within, the inner calling pleading with us to follow our purest heart's desires.

Perhaps you have not followed these desires because you felt they were impossible. You may feel limited in your resources. You may be afraid of the consequences. Perhaps you have made attempts and failed.

Our excuses are many, and, often, there is no convincing us that it can be done. All these lend to us giving up and blocking out our heart's calling. Yet it persists.

However, when you pursue your calling, delving deeply into your greatest heart's desires, you will begin to think intuitively. Your guidance begins to show you innovative means to overcome the challenges blocking your path. Like the Wright brothers taking flight, you overcome your "can'ts."

How Many Traits Do You Have?

- ☐ Unusual childhood?
- ☐ Lucky to be alive?
- ☐ Desire to feel safe?
- ☐ Not afraid to 'fly' your own way?
- ☐ Ever wonder if you were adopted?
- ☐ Trouble making decisions?
- ☐ Difficulty losing weight?
- ☐ Chronic or recurring ailments?
- ☐ Want to run away?
- ☐ Want to escape the world?
- ☐ Under the influence of others' opinions?
- ☐ Heart calling you to action?
- ☐ Driven to keep moving or busy?

Perhaps it is Mrs. Fox who puts it most succinctly.

"We're all different," she says to Ash, putting her paw on his scrawny shoulder. "Especially him." She points at her flamboyant husband, who is wearing yellow- and red-striped pajamas. "But there's something kind of fantastic about that, isn't there?"

Indeed there is, Mrs. Fox. Indeed there is.[1]

---

1. Quoting from the movie, *Fantastic Mr. Fox*, and an article found at http://thekosmo.com/entertainment/outsiders-unite-the-life-and-work-of-filmmaker-wes-anderson

Activating Your Inner Potential

Your First Steps Forward

There are three things—no four—that the ugly duckling did to transform his life.

These are very simple steps that you too can employ. They are so simple and basic, they may surprise you. In fact, you may already be doing them.

First, and most importantly, the ugly duckling could feel the ache and calling in his heart pulling him forward to do what he so longed to do. (Swim) We all have some calling within us and following that call, even if it might be in some tiny, insignificant way at the beginning, is vital in activating your transformation. This calling also compelled the once ugly duckling to suddenly realize he could flap his wings and fly.

The second most important thing the ugly duckling did, was to place himself in the proximity of those who represented what he loved most. Although he did not expect a good outcome in doing so, he bowed his head and humbly swam over to be near the magnificent swans he had come to love.

Put yourself in the proximity to experts who are skilled at what you want to do. Look to be in the company of those who provide encouragement as you spread your wings to fly. If you like to paint, you should be with other painters. If you like to bake, be with other bakers. If you want to build, or hike, or sew, or sing, or any other thing that is calling from your heart to be done, find others who are doing it and be with them.

If your only option is to do so as a bystander, then do it! Be their assistant, their costumer, their typist, their roadie. You never know what opportunities will come up just by knowing the right people. Being with them and in conversation with them will help you in a multitude of ways, and **it is an important component to your success**.

And, if it's something that's never been done before, then find others who appreciate and support what you want to do.

These first two steps will push you forward toward tremendous possibility and transformation, but there are two more.

Transformation

When the ugly duckling stepped into his new persona as a swan, it was a tremendous and instant transformation for him.

Note that 'transformation' isn't a step, rather it is a result of moving forward.

Although it is clear to the observer that the little fellow had been changing all along as he grew, he had no knowledge of this. For him, the true transformation took place in the instant he saw himself for the first time.

I remember in one animated version of the story, whenever the duckling looked down into the water, it would be rippled, thus distorting the view of himself as his mind already had.

There are two kinds of transformation. One is instant. The other takes time. Swans have instant transformations. "Butterflies" take time to emerge from their spun cocoon and fly.

Butterfly people are not big leap people. Butterfly people start out as caterpillars and slowly evolve. First, they chew on it for a bit. They want to fully digest what this leap means, what it will be like to fly in their new world, and how they are going to go about it. Then they begin building it. They carefully spin all the details and, once they have the foundation built, they allow that transformation to gradually take place from deep within their cocoon. However long this may take, when they finally emerge, the transformation is huge.

Butterfly transformations are for the contemplators. It's for the ones who calculate before they leap. They plan it out and they build it. It takes more time, but they feel more confident because they have a support system in place to help them make that leap.

Like the swans, butterflies may not at first realize just how big that transformation will be. They may not realize their full potential. They may not believe what they deeply desire is even possible. Having been a "caterpillar" all their lives, it may not seem possible that they could somehow fly. People around them may constantly remind them that they are caterpillars.

For butterflies, structural changes must take place. For example, a degree must be earned, a business must be built, a health issue has to be healed, a challenging life situation must be resolved. These things take time, effort, dedication, and commitment to the task at hand. If what you need is something like this, go for it! Just know it can't happen immediately. (Yet, aspects leading up to it may appear, as needed, instantaneously.)

Swan people are big leap people. They can shift their perception and are off and running. They are the ones who walk into work one day and say, "I quit." They leave and never go back—no regrets. They use the power of that shift to motivate them to go forward into their next endeavor.

For swans, transformation comes from a mind shift, a change in *perception*. It's about how you approach a problem, how you see yourself and others in your world.

The definition of perception is: "*a way of regarding, understanding, or interpreting something; a mental impression.*" When you change your perception you can change a situation instantly.

How does that work?

In my book, *Hatch – A Change Your Life Guide*, I tell the story about the dirty thermos left on the counter by my younger son. Try as I might, I couldn't get the lid off so I could wash it. That lid wouldn't budge for all the might I put into it.

When I handed it to my older son to help, he asked, *"Why do you want to take the bottom off?"* The bottom?! (What?!) No, I'm trying to remove the top, the lid. . . Or so I perceived.

The thermos had been sitting on the counter *upside down*. I never realized it. My *perception* of the problem was all wrong. Once my perception changed, the solution was instant.

A change in how you perceive yourself, how you allow other's comments and actions to affect you, and how you react to those things, can be changed by seeing them in a different light.

What changes in perception could change your story?

Mark Wolynn writes in his book *It Didn't Start with You*:

> *"My blindness was both literal and figurative. Now I was beginning to wake up, mostly to the fact that I had left a huge mess back home. For years, I had judged*

my parents harshly. I imagined myself to be far more sensitive and human, then they. I blamed them for all the things I believed were wrong in my life."[1]

Wolynn goes on to explain how he began having conversations with his parents and learned more about their experiences and the events that had shaped their lives. Over time, he began to see them in a new way, which, amazingly, also changed his eyesight.

Wolynn's new perspective helped him heal his relationship with his parents and restored his vision. While these changes were not instant, *the moment his perception changed*, the shifts in his life immediately began to follow.

My mother used to reminisce how, as a child, her mother would send her out to sell magazine subscriptions. In those days, you could receive gifts (called '*premiums*') for selling these. Many of the ladies' magazines offered them. My mother hated doing it and likely felt embarrassed, shy, and nervous going door-to-door. She only saw the perception of how she felt doing the selling.

When I think of the story, I am reminded of how my widowed grandmother used her resourcefulness to gather in anything she could to make ends meet. Caught in the grips of the Great Depression without a breadwinner and two young children still at home, she worked tirelessly to feed and clothe her family. She pulled in money by taking in borders, baking pies, doing laundry, mending, anything to bring in a few more dollars.

---
1. *From, It Didn't Start with You*, Mark Wolynn. Penguin Books. ©2017.

Which one would you be more likely to respond positively to in such dark times? An innocent, wide-eyed child standing at your door? Or a disheveled, weary-worn mother of four? Looking at both sides changes my perception of my mother's story.

After my father died, Social Security checks came in my name. My mother would ask me to sign them and give them back to her. I saw it as money that came to me. It was "mine." I felt I could spend it as I chose. (Oh, and the things I could spend it on!) My mother explained that, if I wanted a roof over our head, clothes to wear, and food to eat, I'd better give it to her. She changed my perception. I never questioned her again. Later, as an adult, I marveled at how she managed to pay the bills, pay off the hospital, and provide some fun stuff too. As a youngster, I didn't understand those things.

H.C. doesn't give any great details as to what changed the ugly duckling's perception. He uses the metaphor of seeing himself in the mirrored water. It's there in the reflected pond that he sees himself as he truly is for the first time.

For us, it might take a little more. We must first understand what our perception (or belief) is, then determine if that belief is really true. Not only do we regularly fail to do this, we rarely recognize our perceptions at all.

In my book, *Hatch – A Change Your Life Guide*, I delve more deeply into perceptions and how to change them. However, at its simplest form, just write down what you believe about a situation, then write down other potential possibilities. Is what you believe the only possible answer? Do others involved have a different perception? What do they believe? If other potential answers exist, how do you know that your perception is the matter-of-fact true one?

I like to call myself out on my mistaken perceptions. When I catch myself believing something that may or may not be true, I remind myself, "That's just a belief."[2] I find that just by reminding myself of that can change my perception.

When other parties are involved and you don't see eye to eye, try to understand what the other person might believe. If possible, take time to discover what events or reasoning occurred as a catalyst to create that person's belief. If possible, discuss those presumptions with them. Be willing to listen. Be okay to 'agree to disagree.' You cannot go into any situation hoping to change another person's mind (perceptions or beliefs), but you can try to understand them.

In situations where no discussion can take place, or where it would be futile to do so, you can still try to see the matter from the other person's shoes. In Mark Wolynn's book, he says he has a pair of footprints on his office floor. He asks his clients to stand in them and imagine they are the other person and attempt to feel what they might have felt.

---

[2]. Followers of Access Consciousness call this IPOV or "What an interesting point of view I have." *A Course in Miracles* also attempts to quell mistaken beliefs.

Perseverance

One step not only portrayed in *The Ugly Duckling* tale but in many of the other misfit stories as well, is the ability to persevere through difficulty. The characters keep going no matter how hard the going gets or how bleak their situation appears.

Think of Rudolph the Red-Nosed Reindeer trudging alone through the North Pole snow and ice. Think of Luke Skywalker who has lost his hand and is hanging on an exterior space ladder hoping to be found. And of course, our forlorn ugly duckling survives through a harsh winter and many other trials. These characters hadn't yet stepped into their full selves and power.

Throughout the story, W.C. tries to describe just how bleak the little duckling's plight really was, yet onward he went. Perseverance is the fourth step.

When things got tough for me, I would tell myself, *"wait one more day."* I would keep repeating that day after day until things got better—and they always did. Sometimes it just took time—usually, much longer than I would have liked.

In dark times, it can feel as if there is no end in sight, no way to remedy what needs remedied. Keep going.

At times, it feels as if there could be no possible way to answer the call of your heart. Stay on the path. Some things take time. Sometimes the right elements need to come together. This is where intuition and watching for "signs" play a role.

In times when it feels as if you are stalled or going nowhere or just can't get ahead, understand you may have been held back for a reason. We don't always understand our life situations at the moment they are happening. It's often only in retrospect that you can understand the "why."

Sometimes it feels as if there is a thick plastic shield between you and what you desire. In order to press through that barrier, you have to keep showing up, keep trudging on. (In writing, sometimes I have to force myself to sit in the chair, and write whatever comes out so I can dig down to find the gems.)

Persevere. Keep going forward. One day, one step, one minute at a time.

Back to the Beginning

Let's go back to the beginning where we started, not just in the book, but with ourselves.

You were brought into this world by way of your parents and were raised in an environment that molded you into who you are today. This framework can also be utilized now to help you find your way. I refer to this as, "look back to leap forward."

This is not the place to fully detail this process, but the basis is quite simple. Growing up, the culture, environment, social interaction, challenges, and all that you've experienced, played an important role not only in forming who you are today but also, who your family is or was.

I like to create lists of the people in my life, what their challenges were, what their talents were, what their gifts to me were. These all help me to better understand what has been passed down to me.

History has a way of replicating itself in some form. We may think of this in terms of genetics, but I see affecting us on a much deeper and wider level than just biologically. Maybe dad faced addictions and now you do too. But maybe his was alcohol and yours is food. Maybe mom never felt loved, and now you wonder why you feel alone, even though, unlike her, you are surrounded by a fulfilling family. Many life situations and feelings carry forward when not fully resolved by those who came before.

Digging into your past can help you see these patterns and, by seeing them, you can begin to circumvent them. I like to look at photos of my relatives when I do this. It helps me to connect with them on a deeper level.

Here's a simple method you can try:[1]

Pick a relative in your bloodline. I prefer to start with mom or dad or a central caregiver from your youth. Begin to brainstorm in the following categories. I like to form lists or mind map.

- Skills and jobs held
- Life challenges
- Health challenges
- Key personality traits
- Life happenings that shaped their lives as youths

I also like to create a life timeline, but that is optional.

Looking at all these things, begin to compare them to your own life. Where do you see patterns and similarities in your lives? Which of these patterns are you already aware of? Any surprises?

---

[1] You'll find more detail on this in my *Hatch – A Change Your Life Guide*, or watch for the forthcoming *Marvelous Messages from Your Ancestry* and it's accompanying card deck to learn more.

'Swans' Light Your Way

Think of someone you deeply admire. Their achievements, their character, their values. They may be living or dead, famous or obscure. Think of how they inspire you, in whatever way that may be.

Swans are typically someone who have overcome great odds to step into a leadership role, master of their craft, or who excel at any achievement that endears them to you.

Swans may show up in your life as your favorite actor, musician, author. or artist. They might be a nationally-recognized sports hero. They may be a leader in their industry whether fashion or technology, medicine or education, spirituality or human rights—anything. They might be political activists, world leaders, or martyrs. They may be world icons such as Mother Teresa, Nelson Mandela, the Dalai Lama, or Gandhi.

Whoever they are, when you think of them, does your heart leap? Does a smile rise up from within? Then these individuals are to you what the swans were to the ugly duckling.

> *One evening, just as the sun was setting amid radiant clouds, there came a large flock of beautiful birds out of the bushes. The duckling had never seen any like them before.*
>
> *They were swans; and they curved their graceful necks while their soft plumage shone with dazzling whiteness.*

They uttered a singular cry as they spread their glorious wings and flew away from those cold regions to warmer countries across the sea.

They mounted higher and higher in the air, and the ugly little duckling had a strange sensation as he watched them. He whirled himself in the water like a wheel, stretched out his neck towards them, and uttered a cry so strange that it frightened even himself.

Could he ever forget those beautiful, happy birds!

One key to these luminaries' status as a "Swan" is how they inspire you. Moreover, allow yourself to recognize that something in *you* is what they reflect back. This means you have characteristics within you that you are admiring in them—*even if you don't recognize it as such.* Your fondness for them serves to remind you of the capabilities and calling within.

Years ago, I deeply admired the speaking and teaching skills of one of my mentors. I never dreamed I might be able to teach or speak or write as he did. I had never done anything even remotely close to what he had done. Yet now I have—and there have been many more individuals in my life whom I have admired and who became powerful influences in who I am today. These small achievements are nothing compared to the whole of unlimited potential we all embody.

I have a bulletin board in my office strewn with photos of people I admire to remind me of my potential. I also have these photos in my screensaver so they periodically flash by and inspire me. Take a closer look at the people you admire. One by one examine each one. What is it about them that stands out to you the most?

Dig deeper into what really sparks your admiration of them. Writing it down may help to clarify these traits. Within these sparks, you will find fragments of your potential self, your inner "Swan."

More Ways to Accelerate Your Transformation

- Take some time to meditate or think quietly so the core of what your heart deeply desires is clear to you. This will always be something ultimately beneficial to your life.

- Determine if the people around you are like-minded and if they have your best interests in mind (or their own).

- Learn to accept that you've been given gifts to succeed that transcend what you lack.

- You may have to try different routes, knock on doors, or become resourceful to move things forward. Actions speak louder than wishes.

- Figure out what scares you the most about answering your heart's call. Write it down—that helps to clarify it. Once you can name it, you can tame it. Fear is typically a lack of knowledge. As long as it is an unknown "something" it is ambiguous and scary. Once it's known, you can find a way around it.

- In whatever capacity is open to you, begin to do it. This may be the most important step of all. Understand that by doing it, you will then be able to refine it and evolve it. What it is at the first may not be what it is at the last—and that's okay!

> Look in the mirror and see your higher self, that part of you that is perfect and complete. Stop seeing yourself as the ugly duckling and begin to see the Swan within. The more you nurture the Swan within, the more it will show itself on the outside. It's okay to be humble and to recognize the mastery in others. It's okay to admire them and to applaud. But also learn to see the glimmer of mastery in yourself. Acknowledge your accomplishments. Reward your hard work. Treat yourself with love and respect.

If you do these things, you'll have a great start to answering the deepest callings of your heart. You will be on the trail of a great adventure, and toward the highest and best of your life.[1]

---

1. Watch for the forthcoming book *Marvelous Messages from Your Heart*.

Next Steps

Marvelous Messages from Your Childhood is part of the Heart Level of the Marvelous Messages process. Other levels include the Root (your heritage), Connection (to the Divine), Overcoming Obstacles (blocking your way), and Transformation (ascension)—or more precisely, achieving that "happy place" you've sought for so long.

I recommend you explore the Heart level first, as this will lead you to all else you desire, as you've seen described herein. The Heart level books include this work, *Marvelous Messages from Your Body,* and my forthcoming book, *Marvelous Messages from Your Heart*.

Next, I recommend exploring your roots, as you will uncover some of the innate challenges ingrained within you and the means to overcome them. I explain this in my book, *Hatch – A Change Your Life Guide* or watch for my forthcoming book *Marvelous Messages from Your Ancestry* and its accompanying card deck for more hands-on guidance.

In private coaching with me, we work together through this process to reveal your innate challenges and free your most heartfelt desires. I use my intuitive abilities to part the veil and connect with your ancestry. We explore your challenges, desires, and their core essence on multiple levels. Visit my website to learn more.

In addition, you might consider any of the following options:

- Watch for additional *Marvelous Messages* books coming soon.

- Visit my website for additional articles, audios, videos, resource links, and other materials designed to help you utilize your Marvelous Messages.

- Watch for my interactive classes and coaching.

- Check for my Facebook groups and connect with me via social media.

If you're ready to experience more, visit my website at:

www.MarvelousMessages.com

Last Thoughts

Can I ask a favor? If you enjoyed *Marvelous Messages from Your Childhood* it would mean a lot if you would let your friends know so they can also experience these enlightening thoughts and mind-opening ideas. Most book reading platforms make it easy to click and share.

If you leave a review for the book on the site from which you purchased it, on Goodreads, your own blog, or your favorite social media platform, I would love to read it. Email me the link at **info@saloff.com**.

I would also enjoy hearing about your experiences using any part of my Marvelous Messages™ process. Email me or feel free to post your questions and comments on my website or any of my social media platforms (links are in my bio at the end of the book). Your valuable feedback helps me to evolve my systems so they can better help others.

About Jamie Linn Saloff

Author, teacher, story weaver, spiritual counselor, seer of visions, pathfinder. . . for over thirty years Jamie has taught type-A-driven free spirits how to become happy, healthy, and wealthy by listening to their body groan and their soul weep.

Jamie strongly believes in the inherent power of our ancestry and in *"looking back to leap forward."* She has frequently appeared as a radio personality, guest blogger, and workshop leader. She has written and been featured in countless articles, blogs, newsletters, and newspapers. Jamie has authored twelve books including:

- *Hatch – A Change Your Life Guide*

- *Marvelous Messages from Your Faith: A Simple and Effective Method to Manifest Your Desires and Receive More Answers to Your Prayers*

- *Marvelous Messages from Your Body: Learn the Meaning of an Ailment to Heal Your Life*

- Be sure to watch for other forthcoming works in the Marvelous Messages series of books, including *Marvelous Messages from Your Ancestry* and its accompanying card deck.

View her books on Amazon here: https://amzn.to/3s837aJ

Jamie has trained with many professional practitioners, healers, and coaches including Elaine and Mark Thomas, Tom Cratsley, Donna Eden, Bill Coller, Lisa Williams, Shirley Caulkins Smith, Sharon Klingler, Sig Longren, Joey Korn, Daniel Hardt, (and many more). She is certified Reiki I. She is a minister and multi-certified graduate of Lily Dale's Fellowships of the Spirit.

In her free time, Jamie enjoys needlecrafts, making jewelry, and golf. She spends time studying spirituality, metaphysics, and parapsychology. She is a Mac geek and spends way too much time on the computer. She lives in PA and NY with her husband and a very spoiled cat. She has two grown sons.

Follow Jamie on the web at:

- **Facebook:** www.facebook.com/JamieLSaloff

- **Instagram**: www.instagram.com/jamie_saloff

- **Twitter:** http://twitter.com/JamieSaloff

- **Linkedin:** www.linkedin.com/in/jamiesaloff

What Others Are Saying About Jamie

"My session with Jamie felt like a FASCINATING journey through my body and my issues with chronic pain. She provided me with great insight as to how to move forward in the healing process, and how to "lighten my load." I seriously had one "Ah-ha" moment after another! After our session ended, I sat quietly contemplating what had been revealed to me through Jamie, and I felt totally empowered to take action in finding the balance needed to heal certain areas of my life. I highly recommend working with Jamie!"

~ Joy Phillips, OnceUponAnArchetype.com

"Jamie does something that is very wonderful. When I started talking with her I felt like I was stuck in a dark forest and did not know which way to turn. Jamie very calmly started asking me questions and making some great connections based on what I was telling her. She took me through the bushes and brambles and lead me into the light. I am now moving forward in the direction that is right for me. Thanks, Jamie, You Rock!"

~ LeeAnn Putnam

"Jamie Saloff is an amazing coach! Her insight and intuition mean she has the incredible ability to get to the heart of the matter quickly and come up with workable practical solutions just as quickly. I was struggling with a thorny personal issue and within just one hour Jamie helped me feel lighter, happier and I knew the clear path to resolve the issue. Easy as pie! If you need help sorting out some of the challenges you face—not just a person to vent to—but someone who will help you arrive at real, workable solutions, contact her today! Thanks, Jamie."

~ Denise Michaels, Las Vegas, NV, DeniseMichaels.com

I am grateful to Jamie for her intuitive listening skills and her ability to help me to understand how my body is telling where to focus attention on my life's journey. Her guidance as a medium brought phenomenal comfort to me. I applaud Jamie's skills and appreciate the knowledge, compassion, and excitement she brings to each session. She is a helper, a healer, and a conduit of messages.

~ Carolyn Hilsdon Gilles

www.ingramcontent.com/pod-product-compliance
Lightning Source LLC
Chambersburg PA
CBHW071032080526
44587CB00015B/2578